NBR TODAY's CSR JOURNEY GLOBALLY

AUTHOR
NAVEEN BHATNAGAR

DEDICATION

My beloved Parents Shri. K.P. Bhatnagar & Smt. Savita Bhatnagar are a source of constant inspiration for my works.

They are watching, guiding my innate-self, transforming my works for furthering enshrined noble, altruist cause *E*ffective *E*ducation → an avowed purpose.

Blessings of Almighty, Parents, my Guru's, unwavering love of Family, support, guidance of my Relatives, Friends, above all, avid Reader's community spread across the globe - it would never-ever have been possible for me to deliver knowledge with such ease, alacrity.

OM SAI RAM!
Naveen Bhatnagar- Author
FCS, LL. B, MBA (Finance), PGDM (CL&M), CMA (1),
M. Com
https://www.amazon.com/stores/author/B08CP9SL6W/about

FOREWARD

WE, THE PEOPLE pray for a safe, healthy, prosperous lives of everyone!

With your all blessings, in my career graph, i continue to engage in multi-faceted roles, as has been always, an **Author**, a Mentor, a Professional, on Board in multi-faceted roles such as a **Company Secretary**, Head-Legal, Head-HR, GM-Finance with MNC's inter-alia, **Dell**, **JTEKT**, Hyatt; Indian Leading Conglomerate's →→→→→→ *ITDC, Patna Metro, OPG Power & now with, Pingaksh Group* *https://pingaksh.com/*

CSR Awards (2022-23) Team Review Meeting.... *Photo: this photo is used for representation purposes only.*

NBR TODAY® is an independent, non-partisan work. For NextGen Demystifying Artificial Intelligence, Economics, Environmental & Consumer Law's, Revision of Accounts, Constitution(s), their relevance to your daily lives, including Books for the Students, Professional's, NGO's, Public at large will be of some learning, Value Addition to your chores.

Every effort is made to develop the concept NBR TODAY's CSR JOURNEY GLOBALLY, holistically, culminated in a few pages, possibly in the form a "Ready Reckoner / Digest / Guide".

Photo: this photo is used for representation purposes only.

The purpose of writing this Book NBR TODAY's CSR JOURNEY GLOBALLY is to help ease understanding, knowledge of vast Professionals' fraternity especially NextGen in the Corporates, Elite Class {'*Key Managerial Personnel, Directors*'}, Student's Community, avid Investor's, NGO's & General Public at large. Unearth, unravel this NBR TODAY's CSR JOURNEY GLOBALLY

"Treasure" & many more such Treasure(s) on **Amazon**, **Notion Press & many other platforms Globally**, as detailed hereunder: -

BUSINESS

NBR Today Revision of Accounts →
https://a.co/d/a6UbUkO
NBR Today CGST Digest
NBR Today GST Ready Reckoner
NBR Today MSME Ready Reckoner
NBR Today Insolvency and Bankruptcy Code Ready Reckoner

CONSUMERS
Arbitration Ready Reckoner
NBR Today Consumer Protection Ready Reckoner
NBR Today Motor Vehicles Act Ready Reckoner

ENVIRONMENT

NBR TODAY's CSR JOURNEY GLOBALLY
NBR Today Disaster Management Ready Reckoner

GLOBAL LAWS
We the People: Constitution of the United States
We the People: Constitution of the USA (India Edition)
NBR Today WHO Ready Reckoner

INFORMATION TECHNOLOGY
Demystifying Artificial Intelligence →

REAL LIFE STORY
NBR Today's ITDC: The Untold Story →

PENAL LAWS
Police Act Ready Reckoner
Cr PC Digest
CPC Digest

<u>**SCHOOL BOOKS**</u>
NBR Today Class X Social Science
https://store.pothi.com/book/ebook-naveen-bhatnagar-nbr-today-class-x-social-science-understanding-economic-development/

NBR Today Class XI Business Studies
NBR Today Class XII Indian Economic Development →
https://amzn.in/d/9Ztbse3

<u>**HON'BLE SUPREME COURT**</u>
NBR Today SCJ-HNS Supreme Court Judgements →
https://amzn.in/d/4MSWBZa

NBR Today Sushant Singh Rajput CBI Case →
https://amzn.in/d/0nbRh8E

<u>**FOR WOMEN**</u>
Protection of Women from Domestic Violence Act, 2005
NBR Today Sexual Harassment of Women at Workplace
(Prevention, Prohibition & Redressal) Ready Reckoner
https://www.amazon.com/stores/author/B08CP9SL6W/about
https://nbrtodays.webnode.page/

PREFACE

NBR TODAY® respects your precious yet, invaluable time & supports knowledge sharing.

NBR Today® has taken utmost care to the extent necessary to provide correct, reliable, verifiable information, up to date *(until April, 2025)* in this marvel, NBR TODAY's CSR JOURNEY GLOBALLY. At the same time the Author acknowledges the contribution made by various stakeholders such as Government, Businesses, NGO's, Corporates, Public- who all have been in this Book duly acknowledged, credited for their wonderful achievement, CSR works done. A big, warm thank you all. We sincerely respect your privacy & abide by the same... Thank You All for your overwhelming guidance, support in making this journey a true inspiration for the NextGen.

All possible precaution & care has been taken in this work to avoid mistake/s & omission/s etc. for which the author / editor, publisher and / or the seller/s are in no way responsible.

All disputes are exclusively subject to the Hon'ble Courts in New Delhi in India only. Our maximum liability is limited only to the extent, to return the amount paid & realized from the esteemed Purchaser / Reader of my Authored Books.

———

ACKNOWLEDGEMENTS

Above all, the Author acknowledges invaluable contribution of his Family.

At the same time, special word of thanks & appreciation for the incredible support, advice of fellow professional colleagues in the Corporates, Government Officials & their support Staff, NGO's, Mentors, Relatives & Students on WhatsApp, e-mail, Social Media platform & through their Personal interaction.

They all have been giving, providing support in terms of their invaluable advice, feedback, suggestion for timely correction, updating the contents of this Book. https://www.udtltd.com/csr-financial-reports/

THANK YOU ALL!

In the old era until 1990's, CSR was limited to a select few, top-notch Companies, globally. It was done purely as a voluntary exercise, without any legal, mandatory boundation, binding force.

Hence, it was never raked-up, unless & until Enforcement, Regulatory agencies so sought for it across the globe. There-apart, there were instances to ensure compliance, largely under Companies Act, in India under the aegis of Ministry of Corporate Affairs {'MCA'} in India, which pioneered mandatory, strict regulations therefor.

MCA, for short, allowed CSR allocation, disbursement by a select few Class of Corporates, only for identified, limited purposes, to accommodate compliances under Companies Act & not otherwise. In short, vast strata of the Society, Corporates are, **_still_**, outside its ambit. Still, it's a good beginning, which augurs well in the coming times for the World to emulate, if done in the right earnest.

Under the modern era in India post 1991, also, World-over businesses (post financial misdoings by Parmalat Dairy – early 1990's, Gainax-1999, Enron-2001 Scandal; Satyam -2009; etc.) have grown manifold, also had *extincted*, at a phenomenal speed, become quite cumbersome, fast, loaded with numerous complex compliance issues, on a day-to-day basis. In the Budget 1991, unleashing slew of reforms aimed towards {liberalization, privatization &

globalization}, Dr. Manmohan Singh ji, Finance Minister then had while presenting landmark Budget Quoted French Novelist Victor Hugo that "**_No Power on Earth can stop an Idea whose Time has come_**". The Author too firmly believes it, so also, for the World to take a Leaf out of this Famous French Novelist quote & steer the Ship out of the troubled waters, for sure in next 15 years to see the Mother Earth live in peace, harmony, tranquility, dignity & respect.

Also, with a view to ensure, especially, with India's businesses become competitive with global companies, post Dr. Manmohan Singh reforms unleashed (1991), having a level playing field, fair play, the government of India had promoted "MAKE IN INDIA" an important step in this direction and "EASE OF DOING BUSINESS", coined, promoted the concept "START-UP COMPANY".

In order to give fill-up to this concept, focus of the statutory, regulatory agencies tilted more towards "self-regulation", "exceptions rule" "single window clearance regime" thereby ushering friendlier environment, reposing faith in the Corporates being a responsible, law abiding, compliant Citizens.

As such, major break-through was made under new regime, giving more freedom to run businesses.

Companies are now freer to undertake on purely on voluntary basis, CSR works, apart from the mandatory compliance under Section 135 of the Companies Act, 2013.

On the other hand, in case regulatory bodies find out something grave, seriously wrong-doings committed, fraudulent activities, actions, etc. will act against those which spoil the realm of corporate faith in the such CSR works by the Corporates, NGO organizations, Persons associated in Compliance (or) the like.

As such, all such situations are covered under the new Section 135 which was introduced under the Companies Act, 2013, replacing Companies Act, 1956 altogether in Indian perspective. India is unique, as its mandatory to make contribution under CSR. This idea was coined, developed in India. Now, it's the rest of the World ***to take leaf out of India's success, failures had in its CSR Journey*** and implement them in their respective countries, jurisdictions, as per their need.

NBR TODAY's CSR JOURNEY GLOBALLY is made in simple language, easy to understand by general public at large.

While every effort is made to culminate, present this growing area of practice, undertake projects funded through public resources in the form of Ready Reckoner / Digest / Guide which is made in very simple language, easy to read and understand.

With Technology use, this work can be translated in the language(s) your good-self so choose to read it.

At the same time the Author acknowledges the contribution made by various stakeholders such as Government, Businesses, Corporates, NGO's, Public- who all have been in this Book duly acknowledged, credited for their wonderful achievement, CSR works done. A big, warm thank you all. We sincerely respect your privacy & abide by the same... Thank You All for your overwhelming guidance, support in making this journey a true inspiration for the NextGen.

Hope it is found useful, vital information is captured, purpose is achieved, accomplished.

Readers, kindly do note that the words "Corporate", "Company", "Business-Houses", "Business/es" "Organization/s", etc. are used ***inter-changeably***.

It is clearly understood that no part of this work, book is intended to harm anyone, any institution, government, regulatory bodies, Nation (or) the like (nor) is offensive in any manner whatsoever under extant Laws of the Land.

Still, no work is 100% correct, full proof, which obviously opens many questions, queries, etc. to be addressed. Do the images herein belongs to someone having rights over them, kindly do contact me for the same?

Most humbly seek your sincere, yet honest feedback
+91 9810224073 (*WhatsApp*); +91 8130839020
naveenbhatnagar27@gmail.com

INTRODUCTION

Across the Global Village, over the recent past, say 15-20 years, *we* all, certainly must be witnessing sudden spurt, rush in the activities concentrated in the field of "Sustainable Development Goals (SDG)", "Social Activism", "Socially Accountability", "Social Audit", "Social Stock Exchanges", "Socio-Economic causes", "Corporate Social Responsibility (CSR)", "Protection of Flora-Fona" and the like. https://www.udtltd.com/csr-financial-reports/

Photo: this photo is used for representation purposes only

If your innate self- admit this fact, it will be really interesting, intriguing to Unravel the future Road-map for CSR across the Global Village.

Come along-with Me!

Let's Start walking on this Road called NBR TODAY's CSR JOURNEY GLOBALLY

In the present age, admittedly, we all are living in "Fear" factor in each one ours' Life. This Fear has got different styles, nomenclature, etc. There are reasons for this "Fear Factor" instilled in each of us daily lives, be it "Covid-19 Pandemic", "Wars", "Unstable Leading Economies leading to Recession", "Unforeseen, Unheard Health issues", etc.

There-apart, "Global Warming", Environmental changes & disasters unfolding before our very **E**yes", "Catastrophic Climatic changes" such as Cloud-burst, Rains, Floods playing havoc, Earthquakes, meltdown of Arctic, Himalayas at astonishing speed, Pollution, etc. are becoming a part of our mundane, sagging lives, already saddled with "Fear Factor". Due to Global Warming taking a severe beating, these are obvious Environmental disasters, leave aside, in our daily life's we face Health, Security {Financial & Physical} concerns.

For a layman's understanding, CSR is responsibility towards society by a Company or the like. Is it just an eye wash (or) in reality is there?

With this short introduction, **NBR Today**® explains, with interesting anecdote's showing that CSR has evolved with passing times, more profoundly in recent 10-15 years for sure. Also, its roots were in USA, which were translated in different countries, regions & India in particular has now taken 'Key' Leadership role in this direction. The work though largely Philanthropic, Charitable, Voluntary, etc. (mandatory for a select few Companies in India, China, Malaysia, etc.) has been seeing different, yet difficult times in the evolving economic, social, political situation. Yet, it has been a beacon of hope, especially, for the Corporates, Society, Governments in the Global Village, & more profoundly, the general public, those Individuals, groups, etc. working day & night to see the Mother Earth live another 100 years.

The Author has given real life experiences, verifiable facts, new ideas, interesting, challenging areas of works which makes this work quite intriguing facets of life, corporate culture, ethos which topics are highly readable.

May I take the honors to introduce to You All the **active** Pivot Players in this CSR Journey in the Global Village: -

- Government
- Businesses
- Education Institutions
- Healthcare Fraternity
- NGO's &
- Stock Exchanges
- Finally, the untapped, unnoticed segment, vast reservoir of General Public across our Global Village, who are active, both providing help Voluntarily (*without any favour, reward, expectation in return or the like*), such as financial help (or) their personal belongings (such as Clothes, Utensils, Food) and at times, providing their participation themselves, an avowed Self-less Services called **'Seva' towards → Humanity, Animals, Environment** in the need of the Hour.... Wow! **Hats-Off**.

What of these pivot players do is essentially guided under the aegis of the UN Charter. The Industrial Standards Organization ('ISO'), Council for Economic Priorities Accreditation Agency has put forward Social Accountability ('SA800') Standards for Corporates, etc. to strictly adhere. The idea is to **_collate_**, "Profitability" and "Being Socially Responsible" amongst the vast reservoir of Corporate Entities, both in the Short-Term & Long-Term. If possible, to extend the participants in its cover, which is imperative, need of the hour.

The aim of our _journey_ → NBR TODAY's CSR JOURNEY GLOBALLY is essentially is to **_Walk the Talk_**, pin-point specific areas of concern, looking for plausible answers, finding a defined, yet, definite solution that too in a few minutes, hours, days, but certainly, not in a month or months (or) year or years' time, for sure.

The reason for defining "Time" hereinabove, stems from the fact that time is limited for everyone. On top of it, "Uncertainty" is ruling more professionally, in every sphere of our mundane life now-a-days. The 3rd most important relevant factor, the Driver of any, any, for that matter any CSR Work is "Money". Rest all factors such as, spirit, enthusiasm, dedicated team, plausible projects, corruption, etc. etc. are secondary, or we can admit so, not relevant for our discussion at the initial stages to start any CSR Project.

In this limited time at disposal, bitter experiences in real life are faced by a select few people who struggled to reach the post, attain their cherished destined goals. *Those facing bitter experiences, can really prove to be a game changer, Asset in this NBR TODAY's CSR JOURNEY GLOBALLY Journey*. I make a fervent appeal to all of them to come forward to help us save Mother Earth, yet another 100 years with grace.

Photo: this photo is used for representation purposes only

To name a leading Noble Soul, Saint **Mother Teresa**, known to most of us, Globally. To me a "Living God" then…, as I perceive so…Similarly, **Bhagwan Sri Satya Sai Baba** too. <u>The Author had, in person, in initial stages of his career, met, experienced their company</u>. We all have 2 hands, but for Noble Soul, the hands were infinite, serving the poor, destitutes, people having severe health issues, spreading message of Love, Peace & Harmony, etc. across the Global Village. Anyone who helps in the need of hour is a **True Human**, anyone who gives Life back is a **Doctor**, while, anyone who personally assuages sufferings like a Mother / Father, is above all, arguably, is a **God**.

The burning issues under CSR Journey encompass broad questions about the changing relationship, role, expectations from the Business, Society and Government, Environmental issues, Corporate Governance, the Social and Ethical dimensions of the Management, Globalization, Stakeholders debate, Shareholders and Consumer Activism, changing Political systems and values, ways in which Corporations respond to the new, ever changing social imperatives, institutional, regulatory, and governance issues.

This work is an authoritative review of the research, practical **_Hard-core Experiences_** from verifiable sources, reports, etc. that has both prompted, and responded to, these issues. Bringing together leading experts in the area, it provides clear thinking and new perspective on CSR and the debates around it. It is divided into Eight {'**08**'} Key Sections: -

* Introduction
* Challenges
* Key Players
* CSR Management
* CSR in Indian perspective
* Case Studies
* CSR in the Global Context {in the Underdeveloped / Developing / Developed Economies}
* Future perspective

This work of mine aims to target cutting-edge developments in mindset of the Businesses, Society,

Governance, managing these Stakeholders (Key Players), challenges of Business Ethics thereby making CSR a sustainable work, Corporate Governance & host of other issues engulfing them. There apart, there are other areas which are not essentially in the realm of Corporate Business model, such as Social-work, Philosophy, Education, Psychology, Philanthropy, etc.

This work should address, enthuse young students, teaching community be it in the Colleges, Schools, Professional bodies, Research, working class such as NGO's, working Professionals, Doctors', Economists', Corporate Leaders', etc. and a vast untapped segment, the self-less humans...whom we all see, admire in and around us, a separate *C*lass altogether.

Examples: -

❖   Crossing of Road by Old being assisted, escorted.

❖   Most of us have been witnessing road rage accidents. Someone comes from nowhere & gives first-aid, water, etc. to accident victim, at the place of mishap, natural disasters such as floods, cyclone, earthquake, volcano, etc.

❖   Giving Food at Road-side, in the Parks, within the Apartments / Colony's, etc. to the unattended Cows, Monkeys, Cats, Dogs, Ants, etc. & other animals on frequent intervals in a week, month, etc.

❖   Helping hand to the old people in Old Age Homes by Volunteers.

Photo: this photo is used for representation purposes only.

❖ Counselling people faced trauma, mental imbalance, anxiety, etc.

❖ Students offering voluntary services at the road side, railway junction, bus/ metro's educating people not to fall prey to touts, unscrupulous, mischievous, anti-social elements, also, these students are found making reports on traffic, strata, speed & a host of other parameters, etc.

❖ Pooling of Food, Clothes, etc. for Poor & Under-privileged done by a particular segment of society, group of senior people, more particularly through delivery vans at pre-destined location, at hotels, convention Centre, marriage venue, etc.

❖ Voluntary Education to Children, Extra-curricular Activities such as tailoring, stitching, Computer skills for Employment, Rehabilitation programs run for Drug addict, minor thefts, etc. under guidance of the local police, etc.

❖ Planting of Trees, etc. especially by the school children, colleges, voluntary organization, etc. to avoid soil erosion & maintain ecological balance... and more to add every moment across this Global Village......

......A Big Hug, Thank You ALL....

For any CSR project, what "IMPACT" it has made on our Society is important. At the same time, impact's assessment is to made as soon as possible. Also, what "LESSONS" were learnt therefrom are equally pivot.

CHALLENGES

Corruption:

It is experienced, most often, more than 50% of the available funds for CSR are directly or indirectly swindled, taken in some (or) other reasons under the garb of adjustment, collusion, long-term benefit, ***deliberate expenses shown***, kickbacks, personal use, misinformation, personation / using funds in name of persons not existent / non-living, use for projects which ultimately interests select few (not for the society), or worst, even, directly asking, taking cash (or) in kind reward for arranging CSR funds from the Government, Corporates, etc. This is a global menace, which needs to be addressed by the United Nations.

It is highly unethical, cheating, but, this ill can be lessened, but cannot be eradicated totally from the CSR funding of the Projects across the global spectrum.

To assuage the plight of needy, deserving, there should be concerted efforts to eradicate this menace from the Society.

Devoted Work-force:

It is often seen, under pressure, enthusiasm, spur of moment, etc. CSR works are undertaken. With passing time, due to shortage of funds, ageing, untimely Death of the Leadership, Heath issues, other gainful opportunities, some times force from the local people / anti-social elements, etc. the Devoted workforce gets distracted, or even worst, stoppage of the CSR program altogether.

To address this issue, it is imperative, apart form dedicated work-force, there is need to broad-base the management of the CSR Projects, with involvement of the Government machinery in its functioning (wherever necessary, need basis). _Also, to make it a people's movement, by making them a part of the Leadership, decision making like Shareholders {Minority Shareholders, etc.} in a Company_.

Photo: During chilling winter nights in around Delhi, Noida, Gurugram, Ghaziabad (India) on road-side 2 p.m., most often, distributing blankets to the needy. This photo is used for representation purposes only.

Funding:

For any CSR works, projects to be successful, having sustainability, etc. its important that there are Funds at its disposal at frequent interval/s. Without this, the whole project gets derailed. The funds requirement is both Capital nature (Infrastructure development, maintain it), as well as, Revenue nature (day to day expenses such as electricity, water, medicines, food, clothing, etc. need).

Government Support:

Its very important that the CSR Projects are implemented, reviewed, registered, periodically monitored, etc. at the helm of Government department. The purpose is there is accountability, benefits reaches the needy, there is no malpractice such as cheating, collusion to evade funding & diversion of the funds, the projects can be sustainable with aim to reach the poorest of the poor. Also, in those CSR projects aimed to maintain Environment balance, etc. it will be very important that Government monitors the progress of the funded projects. At Global level, it helps funding from the international organizations & see its utilization, progress on real time basis under watchful eyes.

Celebrity Culture:

Across the global village, it is experienced that there is a "celebrity culture" issue such as those CSR projects blessed with leading names, celebrities, 'gurus', people in the limelight, etc. often take the major share of the cake i.e., funding either from the government, or from the public at large. This notion should be dispelled, funding broad-based, rather, not limited to a select few individuals, institutions or the like.

In brief, those who are capable, able to perform in CSR should be blessed, and rightfully funding at their door-steps, so that they are never short of funds looking *helter-skelter* for funding their identified CSR works in times, hour of need.

Another thought running across mind is to earmark certain number of CSR projects, already in operation to the Leadership in the aided, projects in limelight, reckoning, etc. which have either been blessed so, have been privileged select (not the general public) to access such funds at ease, etc. In this direction, a very good work done at Dell crosses my mind, where the Author was heading its India's Legal & Company Secretarial Department. **https://www.dell.org/apply/** Public too can access this link, benefit by deploying funds for a Social cause, etc.

———

KEY PLAYERS

- **GOVERNMENT**

The government efforts help assure, support CSR projects, in the field of Social Causes, Environmental concern by providing (financial support, administrative support in terms of research reports, data, manpower, seminars, conferences, awards, nominating goodwill ambassadors, etc.).

Photo: Author, representing his Company before several thousand audience, making CSR Contribution for this Noble cause in New Delhi, India. This photo is used for representation purposes only.

The Government also spearheads role the field of drafting policy, regulatory framework for CSR policy implementation by the private sector organizations recognizing works of excellence, setting up of code of conduct, corporate governance reporting in the annual reports of corporates, etc. Most often, these compliances are made on a voluntary basis across the globe. However, in India, under the Companies Act, its mandatory for a select class of companies to strictly adhere law, rules & regulations governing CSR.

The role of any government for that matter, essentially, pertains to promoting CSR works (most often, it is seen that the celebrities such as Film Stars, Business Tycoons, etc. services are utilized to promote causes).

In the recent past, if we recall, refresh our memories, during Covid-19, may be still earlier, HIV prevention projects, epidemics, etc. eradication, safe practices, vaccination camps, etc. were promoted by noted Film

Stars in India such as megastar **Amitabh Bachchan**. In India, most of us recognize ***Do Boond Zindagi Ki*** campaign i.e. to take 2 drops of polio vaccine, that was unleashed in recent past towards totally eradicating, making India polio free, under the aegis of **UNICEF** program.

From USA -**Bill Gates**, Gates Foundation, **Warren Buffett**, **Tata Trusts** CSR funding several Universities across the leading Global Universities such as Harvard Business School. Again, **Angelina Jolie**, Actress for long has been a goodwill ambassador for United Nations High Commissioner for Refugees. She personally looks after several social works world-wide (be it to help refugees & displaced people, poverty alleviation program).

The **European Commission** has for long promoted the role of CSR in public lives. It defined CSR as "*a concept whereby companies integrate Social and Environmental concerns in their business operations and in their interaction with their Stakeholders on a Voluntary basis*". **Nova Nordisk Foundation** focuses on Medical treatment & Research, etc. to name a few prominent names globally, which comes across our mind.

In brief, any CSR Project having ramifications of national (or) international magnitude, scale, etc. are taken up by the Government with the help of the leading celebrities, their organizations, so that the benefits reach the target audience, most sought-after strata, class of people, may be in some cases, the affected geographical resources (such as Dams, Mountains, etc.).

In Africa, mostly (poor) countries, which are typically myriad in poverty, frequent fights, health disasters, etc. making it a nightmare to live in peace & harmony. There are frequent gun battles, oppression of the minority, females, children, old people. UN peace-keeping force with support from the participant countries restore them by providing security, food, medical care, shelter, etc. Also, India's efforts are praise-worthy, its National Disaster Response Force **(NDRF)** – largest force globally handling disasters, is doing splendid works in the field of saving life, especially during Covid-19, Natural Disasters, last week Earthquake in Myanmar (erstwhile Burma), Indonesia, etc. https://www.ndrf.gov.in/ Jai Hind. In this direction, at the UN level, United Nations Office for Disaster Risk Reduction (UNDRR) are praise-worthy. They have highlighted concern about dwindling resources, political priorities, etc. making the relief tasks challenging, etc. We all must come forward and help UNDRR in its efforts to give timely help to the needy. https://www.undrr.org/our-work/history

Photo: this photo is used for representation purposes only. https://www.udtltd.com/csr-financial-reports/

- **BUSINESS**

Businesses have a key role in the CSR arena across the globe. In fact, Business acts as a catalyst for change in the Society. They help Society realize its values, principles, belief towards making the place more hygienic, safer, healthy environment, much more employment opportunities to the locals in around them. These changes can be in the field of moral values, education, health, help the poor, old, food, maintain ecological balance, etc. The task is uphill, daunting, but, not unachievable. Together with concerted minds meeting, proper strategy formulated & implemented in the right Ernest will surely give positive results, targets set. Lot many Corporates have done excellent work in this direction. For Example, Reliance Group in India came up wildlife, Animals protection, preservation plan into action, now a reality named "**Vantara**" in Jamnagar District in Gujarat. Again, French Company "**Danone**" in Food business focused on nutrition, social innovation, healthier habits for eating in the Society, Environment benefit, etc. at large. Similarly, **"Toyota"** has helped more sustainable transport solutions for the benefit of the society, across the globe. **"Adidas"** has helped maintain Human Rights, achieve climate-neutral target by 2050. Bharat Forge in its CSR statement put "*The Society has contributed so much to our Growth over the last 50 years. We, in return, should take actions for its betterment.*" The limit is ever growing in various facets of life, is really commendable, laudable.

- **EDUCATION INSTITUTIONS**

Schools, Colleges, Universities, Skill Development programs, etc. play a very important role in shaping the Society towards CSR targets, both directly and indirectly. The direct impact is made in the mind-set set of the teaching community, teachers, etc. who benefitted a lot in development of *Self*, on a sustainable basis. It goes without saying when anyone is focused towards Society upliftment, Moral values, Health, Sanitation, planting Trees, saving Animal life (giving food, shelter, medical attention), etc. it automatically infuses a sense of belonginess, commitment, mutual respect, etc. All these values are instilled amongst the *T*eaching community, **_which has for sure a Multiplier impact_**, effect on the *T*aught, obviously several Hundreds of Student who directly come under their learning skills, benefit & emulate these across the Society at a mass scale. At the same time, it has helped to bring strong bonding which in India is often told: -

"**_Guru Brahma Gururvishnuh Gururdevo Maheshwarah_**

*<u>**Guruhsakshat   Parabrahma   Tasmai   Shrigurave
Namah**</u>*"

Guru is Brahma Himself. He is Vishnu and He is also
Shiva (Maheshwar). Guru is Parabrahma (Supreme God
or the Absolute Truth). With this Knowledge, I (salute)
offer my Obeisance (to obey, respect) to the Guru.

One classic example to quote from a very recent visit of
World Leading Guru **Sri Sri Ravi Shankar** of <u>***Art of
Living***</u> program held during February, 2025 in Delhi. The
Author was invited to witness the huge gathering very
closely seek his blessings & benefit therefrom amongst
others there.

Photo: actual photo taken by the Author in Art of Living event besides Sri Sri Ravi Shankar.

The real reason was huge gathering of over 1,000 Teachers across Delhi in India assembled at the venue as Volunteers, to help conduct of the program smoothly. This experience was really encouraging, especially for the Students, who read, watched on TV their real-life Hero's *(Teachers)* performing Services at this mega event, for 3 days. The laudable object of CSR is best seen at the program, where Teachers, standing full day in **scorching**

<u>**heat**</u>, helped guide people in thousand numbers come and have blessings, learn skills from the Noble soul, thereby sending message of Peace, Harmony, etc. which is the essence of the Life. A big thanks to the people, police, volunteers, transport support, Delhi Metro, etc. who had made the program *see the light of the day spreading peace, harmony, at the same time helped develop inner-self, conscience doing "Sudarshan Kriya" to be a better Human Being.*

This is one such classic, real life example spreading aroma of love, peace across crores in the Global Village. Equally, there are several others, Teachers to emulate, such as Saint Pope John XXIII, Pope St. John Paul II, His Holiness Dalai Lala, Sri Satya Sai Baba. I am for sure, there are Hundreds, Thousands, Lakhs of such examples set by the Teaching community across the Globe to learn, emulate in our daily life, to bring peace, betterment of the Society at large. It will be really interesting to learn many such more experiences by each one of us, at whatsoever way of life we are living.

In the words of Saint Kabir, poet, "<u>Guru Govind dao khade Kake lage paye Balihari Guru apne Govind diyo bataye.</u>"

A Child should bow down to his / her TEACHER, if both God & Teacher are standing in front. Teacher has taught values, brought light, wisdom to see God, without whom it was impossible to see God.

In Indian Value System, for Ages, Teachers are so Respected. These Values are imbibed, which should be followed by each one of us to be a good human being which makes a mark change in our Life, brighter tomorrow in and arounds us.

- **HEATHCARE FRATERNITY**

Healthcare Fraternity, encompassing Hospitals, Doctors, Nurses, Attendants, Paramedics, Medical Education Institutions, Colleges, Laboratories, Pathology, Medical Stores, Chemists, Ambulances, Pharma Companies making medicines {*Merck & co.,* ***Pfizer, Ranbaxy, Novartis, Dr. Reddy's Laboratories, Astra Zeneca, GSK, Johnson & Johnson, Takeda Pharma, Ship Healthcare, Japan Industrial Partners Inc., Sun Pharma, Cipla, Lupin, Zydus, Bharat Biotech, Serum Institute, etc***.}, doing round the Clock Research, Other Companies too who make Medical instruments, machines such as Scanning, MRI {General Electric, etc.} & a host of all ancillary & support functions associated in around Healthcare fraternity round the clock, in need...***A Big Hug***...Love You All from the bottom of Heart. _The Author had 5 near-death incidents, experiences in his Life_. Healthcare, Doctors, Unflinching Love of His Family, above all, GOD Divine Blessings, had made him stand & present these works amongst the Global Village Family.

Amongst rest other key players, Healthcare Fraternity stands apart, focuses on CSR works & equally important, very critical role to play in the CSR works across the globe. Covid-19 Pandemic, in the recent past has been one of the best examples for everyone across the globe to vouch. Hospitals, Doctors, Nurses, Para-Medical support staff, Ambulance, etc. Salute to then......every second we breathe, live life to the full....... largely because of the relentless efforts of the Healthcare fraternity using technology tools to leverage medical facilities to the needy.

The idea of CSR by Healthcare Fraternity is a part and parcel of the Services rendered by them towards the Society, Community in around them. Health Industry essentially looks after those in need, especially, requiring medical attention, etc. Those able to avail such Services from the Healthcare Fraternity have resources, means, etc. to pay in return. However, in those cases, especially, in urgency, poor, serious health issues requiring immediate attention, chronic diseases, fatal accidents, mental trauma, etc. which Medical services are essential & money is a Secondary consideration. In most of these cases, as a Humane Cause, Moral, Ethical Duty, the NGO's, Corporate's, Social Organizations, even the General Public through Social media platform, etc. come forward to make invaluable "Contribution", in any form be it Money, Non-monetary, in kind Services, etc. to the needy. We all must have read, seen TV, Newspapers, etc. about Accidents in Aeroplanes, etc.

Do hope we All are on the same-page, same-footing. Correct!

In most of the cases, apart from the First Aid, Over the Counter {OTC} Drugs, Medicines, etc., often Doctors, Specialist come forward to give Voluntary Help, Assistance, Attention, etc. to the needy when called, asked for by the Flight Staff on-board.

Photo: this photo is used for representation purposes only.

Healthcare Fraternity looks after CSR in many varied perspectives such as inhouse, outdoor works. Also, it could be for short-duration, long lasting such as Old Age Homes, etc. where Doctors frequently visit and attend the medical needs of old people, who often are alone, without any support, help of the family, etc. All these, essentially are "Being Humane" side of Healthcare Fraternity, who are "LIVING GODS" ......God Bless them ALL from the core of our Heart's......Love U All.

In brief, all these Healthcare Fraternity Family have a very deep-yet, life long values, instills, reposes faith, public view, loyalty, etc. amongst the Community, Society. It goes in a long way towards augmenting World Health Organization's (WHO) laudable causes, Social Determination of Health (SDOH), which essentially dwells around each one of us surroundings, socio-economic considerations having deep impact, effect on us.

Across the globe, CSR is mostly a voluntary process undertaken by the Corporates. However, India has pioneered the CSR initiative as a Compulsory, Mandatory initiative for the select few Corporates under the Companies Act, 2013.

It is not far off, when this initiative will be expanded, to benefit the larger section of the Society's need reaching out to the most needy, poor, etc., yet, broad-based & above all → Time is the essence, i.e., results delivered in least time.

Also, there is universal practices to follow, emulate under CSR by the Healthcare Fraternity. There is no one size-fits-all formula, theory. Every Healthcare Fraternity's Organization can work, perform CSR services, in their respective field of work, not essentially, directly attending the needy, but will ultimately aims to benefit the needy person.

- **NON-GOVERNMENTAL ORGANIZATION'S ('NGO')**

To a large extent, the NGO's work goes hand-in-hand with the Healthcare fraternity. There are numerous examples, especially in the field of CSR which Healthcare fraternity has been in the fore-front, ably supported by the NGO's, what-so-ever be the compelling circumstances, need of the hour, etc. they have all come to help the needy most often, not the greedy.

Examples, in real life experiences had by the Author have been witness to Devastating Floods playing havoc in hilly area around Kedarnath, Uttarakhand (India) in June, 2013 leaving loss of several thousands of people, including, a very dear Professional Friends Wife → still missing, untraceable by the local administration.

This is one of lakh & lakhs of people who across the global village have lost their loved ones, dear family members, close friends in the tragic natural disasters (Earthquake, Floods, Cloud-burst, Forest Fire, etc.). This is one of the several CSR Works which often go unnoticed for over a period of time. To run institutions of like-minded people, making concerted efforts, develop a mechanism for finding the misplaced, restore them to their Family, even, Animals lost, are a part of the affected lot.

There-apart, there are many children, women (young), Old (Men), etc. who are often misguided, misplaced, misinformed and are abducted, leave their families, etc. These strata are most vulnerable for misuse, fall prey to illicit trade, etc. Apart form the local Police authorities, the CSR teams can take a lead, help develop platform, work on social media, canvass door-to-door, etc. to help locate the misplaced, abducted people, alongside, assisted by the local authorities, agencies, police, etc. This will not only help reduce cost of the Police Department, across the length & breath of the Country giving advertisement in the leading newspapers, putting posters, etc. saves their time & divert attention to much more important work (policing, law & order, etc.).

When aged 16 years, the Author was struck in Floods for over 1 month in childhood days in Dowleswaram Village, East Godavari District in Andhra Pradesh (India). He has been actively participant as Bharat Scouts & Guides Voluntary Social Service Institution then, helping the displaced, poor, animals, etc alongside, the government machinery, Doctors, etc.

Photo: Dowleswaram, Andhra Pradesh. This photo is used for representation purposes only.

Similarly, Tsunami in Indian Ocean affecting 12 countries, Japan in 2004, 2011, respectively taking huge loss of lives, animals, surrounding areas habitat, environment, etc. 7.5 magnitude earthquake in Turkey in 2023 leaving lakhs displaced, severe health issues to counter, deadly wild-fire, volcanos across the globe. In all of the natural disasters, etc. the Healthcare fraternity was in the fore-front, on humane cause, helping the need in the hour or grief. Very recently, on 28th March, 2025, Myanmar {'Burma' until 1989} & Thailand witnessed horrific 7.7 magnitude earthquake, killing several humans, animals & huge economic loss to their respective economies.

Across the globe, apart from the efforts of the Healthcare fraternity, many leading names, voluntary associations, institutions, etc. are a few names to reckon, such as, but not limited to **Red Cross, Rockefeller Foundation, CARE, CRY, CRS, International Federation of Red Cross and Red Crescent Societies, Amnesty International, Medecins Sans Frontiers, OXFAM International, Beit Al Khair Society, Dubai Charity Association, UAE Water Aid Foundation,**

GlobalGiving, Qatar Fund for Development, Charity Miles, Reliance Foundation, Tata Trusts.

Let us not forget the invaluable contribution of the Government Department, their organizations developed, dedicated Teams such as NDRF (in India), also, many such Agencies across the Global Village.

- **STOCK EXCHANGES**

The Author firmly believes upon his real-life CSR experiences had, and otherwise, etc. that the Stock Exchanges are the _**only Ray of Hope**_ for supporting the CSR works, on purely Voluntary basis, other than, making appeal, going halter-skelter, making presentations before Corporate Houses to make charity, philanthropic contribution, etc. to funding CSR works.

India, has once gain taken the lead in this direction. Under the aegis of the Securities regulatory authority i.e., the Securities & Exchanges Board of India {'**SEBI**'}, the Social Stock Exchanges has started working, making a meaningful contribution. Fulfillment of laudable objects, Social-Development Goals, Sustainable Development

Goals (SDG), also called, Global Goals were adopted by the United Nations {'UN'} in the year 2015.

The CSR, non-for-profit organizations initiative & simultaneously raising of Funds from the Public for a cause will be litmus test. The flip side, real challenge to raise Funds is to the small, marginalized CSR Projects will be real game changer. Coming 5 years will validate our understanding, whether our assumptions were right (or) wrong.

This platform is a real, true ***blessing in disguise*** to fund, support CSR projects across the length, breath of the Country. Basis, the experiences, results, etc. the World can ***take a leaf out of India's Success stories, Bad experiences had, etc***. and promote the CSR cause in their respective jurisdictions, countries, region, etc. Obviously, with the intent to bring about sizeable changes in their Society Values, address genuine causes, verifiable & accountable CSR projects.

Across the global village, in South Africa, New Zealand, UK, Canada, Jamaica, Brazil, Singapore & many such more social, philanthropy cause institutions are in offing, there were many such platforms which are active in this direction.

———

CSR MANAGEMENT

From the bitter experiences had {*Personal, while working, on-board with several Corporates, MNC's, as also, as an Entrepreneur, Lastly, as a Common-man*} over the past several decades, *as discussed in this work*, it is very important to have a defined road-map. Adherence to defined timelines, flagging upon reaching particular milestone, etc. towards the CSR Journey, so that, there is active participation of various stakeholders, public, government, etc. (other than they very Corporate undertaking CSR work.

The next 'Key' milestone is having reasonable, yet assured, Source(s) of Funding at disposal to meet the Expenses (initially, as also, for couple of months say, for 5-6 months to sustain CSR works (in short-run projects); 3-4 years (for long-run projects).

The final 'Key' factor is much more relevant to make the CSR works sustainable, evenly operate → to have identified, yet, dedicated work-force about 5 to 7 people atleast, for small projects, which can gradually over time increased, depending upon scale of operations, number of people to attend, etc. The Legal framework for CSR work should be a registered Trust only, otherwise, there are chances the work may not be sustainable due to some or the other reasons, as experienced.

Basis above norms, the Management of CSR show, essentially, *pro bono*, will be in order, sustainable, scalable & plausible.

CSR is essentially funding social cause projects by the private sector Companies or the Corporates. However, in Indian context if we were to see, it also covers the **Public Sector Undertakings {'PSU'}** owned by the Government. Also, in respect of funds left unutilized during any particular period, then, its mandatory for those select Corporates to remit, transfer this short-fall, left-over allocated CSR Funds the Government. This is a broader definition, explanation for the ambit of CSR Funds utilization. From a CSR Management perspective, the Companies should holistically, ideally look at, examine its own strengths, value chain, resources at its disposal (be it money, men, material, machinery); the ultimate beneficiary (be it Animals, Humans or the Environment) impact, affect from the CSR projects done. The ultimate genesis of the CSR project is what Objectives, Principles were laid and what, to what extent these were achieved.

In this process, research, analytical tools, data compilation & its dissemination, etc. working on MS Excel, specialized software by use of Oracle program, etc. helps ease those

CSR works spread across the length & breath of the defined territory may be at the district level, State, Country, etc. These tools are imperative, very useful statistical tools for any CSR project on a sustainable basis & benefit reaches the farthest most.

There-apart, Corporates should examine the vision, objectives for which it is established. This will largely decide the road-map, direction for CSR works. Also, the identified society, strata to be addressed, allocate men, material, etc. for the identified CSR tasks, implement & review the outcome of the CSR Projects (completed, in transition, yet to start, etc.).

Mathematically, to understand CSR works real value, we use ideal discount rate {as per industry yardstick, benchmarks set, etc.} for the number of years the project is undertaken, basis benefits, deducting therefrom the cost involved therein. Globally, there are many other benchmarks for CSR Projects such as Dow Jones Sustainability Index, London Benchmark Group Index (LBG), QLD Index, etc. which goes a long way to have visibility, recognition, funding of couse. India, recently has set-up Social Stock Exchanges, with several Companies listed therein & raising Funds for Social causes, etc. This platform will go in a long way too to help evaluate CSR projects intrinsic value; value addition made towards betterment of the Society & other parameters therefor.

One must not forget the fact that any Corporate is working for Profits. Profits earned over a period of several years, translates, becomes a Wealth. Again, still further for many more years, decades, continued Profits create huge reservoir called "Reserves & Surplus"→ in legal terms (**_Lasting Legacy, for a common man, woman to understand_**).

__Photo: this photo is used for representation purposes only.__

This is the full vision, dream for that matter name any big Business House across the Global Village, be it Reliance, Johnson & Johnson, GE, Airbus, P&G, Tata's, etc. the list is growing. The point to make is profit comes from Business operations, be it Manufacturing, Services, etc. The recipient of these services rendered by the Corporates is the public at large, government institutions, companies, house-holds, businesses, etc. In effect, as per established research, those Corporates making CSR, garner a better premium as compared to others.

Also, in the long run, these Corporates benefit in Profits generation at a faster pace. In effect, the benefits of CSR work go a long way in establishing, positioning the Corporates in a respected stratum in the Society.

As such, CSR Management ultimately helps Corporates give back to the Society in and around it in a meaningful, yet, on a sustained basis. At the same time, it helps foster moral, ethical values, cherished values, principles amongst its staff to follow, who do not switch jobs most often. It enhances, improves the image of the Corporates amongst the general public, also at the government level. As such, there are more non-monetary gains, apart from monetary gains, especially in the long-run.

Infosys is one such classic example which the Author can vouch. Its initial CSR Journey, Road-map and the present position, is future road-map, etc. all aligned. There were frequent Cricket matches organized by it with the Government (Ministry of Electronics & Information Technology) officials, staff, etc. in Delhi in early 1997-98, when, Infosys started working much more in public glare. This is how proximity with the political dispensation, inroads were established, also, CSR works, a cherished thought for this group. Another favorite sport is Golf, Horse Race, etc. which Clubs were frequently visited by the Corporates to make best use of social gatherings, causes beneficial to them & promote CSR works, making presentation before the select few who's-who {leading names} in the industry.

It may not be out of place to mention here that *m*ost of the top layer Corporates across the Global Village are in the CSR works, **very aggressively pursuing it**, very avidly following its "***Growth Map***" to maintaining their LEGACY across the Society.... for a Noble, Cherished Cause obviously.

A word of caution, CSR is meant to translate benefits to the Society, Environment in and around the Corporates. Anything done with intent to malice, "greenwashing" might land up in turmoil, ruining the Business prospects for the Corporate. In most recent discussions across the Globe, whether CSR work expectation and "Over-work" has any nexus?? Is it good or bad??? Certainly, it is BAD, as per extant research reports, which affects the demographic cult, family system (no urge to have children). This is one of the Key areas which Corporates should energize their skills, focus, rather than, in mad rush to reach the top, epitome of ideal Organization, while its people, in this journey not happy, not satisfied, not content, not in the pink of health either.

———

CSR IN INDIAN PERSPECTIVE

Over the years, there were many bodies, institutions, government department(s) etc. addressing the need for CSR in India, on a purely "Voluntary" "Unstructured" basis "Philanthropy" works. All of these CSR projects were undertaken purely on a voluntary basis, "need basis" if we were to use for more emphasis, clarity, etc. without any legal recourse, even, for the PSU's, which essentially follows, are under administrative directions, control of the Department of Public Enterprises {'DPE'} under the Ministry of Finance, https://dpe.gov.in/en issuing guidelines, notifications, circulars, etc. from time to time for compliance on voluntary, advisory basis, at times more stringent & was prevalent then.

Apart from the Private Sector's participation, if we were to discuss the role, contribution made by the Government, PSU's in the CSR? To a large extent, **HUGE EFFORTS** has been made under the advisory guidance, control of the DPE. The DPE has issued guidelines, as discussed above, for compliance by the PSU's especially in the areas of "*School Education*", "*Healthcare*", "PSU's to identify, *Select Theme/s* for CSR works to be undertaken during each year", the idea of "**Aspirational Districts**" was coined, has been taken up very aggressively in the recent past say about 10 years or so.

The focus of PSU's has been that the CSR projects benefit reaches on a broad basis, to the poorest, development of the Social Welfare, fabric, across the length & breath of the Country, on ***most equitable basis***, without any favour, non-discrimination for race, color, class, creed, sex, religion, place of birth, or the like. This has been enshrined in the Constitution of India under Article 15.

Keeping UN's Sustainable Development Goals {'SDG'} in mind, the Government of India had taken lead & put a regulatory framework for CSR framework. Then, Companies Act, 2013 came into existence. It now made it mandatory for **'earmarked'** Companies to make CSR contribution in the designated projects.

Photo: this photo is used for representation purposes only.

In this direction, MCA has been given the ***prime responsibility*** under the framework of law, which in-turn took the lead, pivot national body which is taking care of CSR in the right ernest, now onwards. Erstwhile Companies Act, 1956 did not contain any provision regulating CSR, nor for any identified funding for it.

In India, there was hardly any statistics available in the field of CSR in public domain. The Government arm,

Indian Statistical Institution has data, but not decipherable for public use. MCA has now made a public platform namely HTTPS://WWW.CSR.GOV.IN which gives wide gamut of reports, which is indeed laudable. For past 2-3 years, there are in-depth discerning analytical reports, etc. available for public debate. However, there is lot to be done in this direction, such as CSR benefits really cascading to the grass root level, common man benefitting in "substance", data-bank to be more realistic, reflective of actual state of affairs in substance, inclusive, detailed / exhaustive {especially, for top 1 to 3 funded projects}, open for public scrutiny, examination to pass real "litmus" test.

One small suggestion to make, let the Comptroller & Auditor General of India {"**CAG**"} Audit be introduced selectively, for the information on this MCA's portal, public view, access, after all its all public's hard-earned taxable money. Correct!

It will have more meaningful, realistic information; giving more teeth to the MCA to be stricter in its enforcement of law in letter & spirit. Just for information of the Readers, CAG Audit for the PSU's is already mandatory, as also, selectively introduced in other areas where there is hue & cry, which also covers the CSR Expenditure made by them. However, for the Private Sector, there is no such a mandatory Audit, which raises eyebrows. This will surely take its best course & bring righteous works in front.

Another, suggestion, there should be single regulatory authority, *albeit*, SEBI, DPE, etc. to be guided by MCA diktat only. Overlapping, over-reaching another territory should be avoided, stopped altogether, which made CSR a laughing stock in the eyes of the Public, at-least, to some extent now lessened.

For Example, all Income Tax matters in India are only regulated by the Income Tax Department, which is under the aegis of the Ministry of Finance, Government of India. What ramifications, implications, etc. arise, if so-ever, there is Income Tax Departments raid, Notice received from it by a common man? Obviously, the answer is "Sleepless Nights". Its ridicule that hard-earned "Profits" of corporates portion of it earmarked towards CSR, mandatorily, or voluntarily remaining un-answered, not used in true letter & spirit for its manifested, cherished purposes "SERVICE TO MANKIND, PROTECTION OF

ENVIRONMENT FROM ANY FURTHER DEGRADATION".

Another suggestion, major portion of the CSR spending of Corporates goes into their earmarked projects, within their own Company, Group, etc. This needs to be corrected, broad-based by participation in Projects with help of Government support, PPP model, etc. so that there is no malpractice, to stop diversion of funds not related to CSR, curb wastage, etc.

One more suggestion, it is experienced larger chunk of CSR expenditure is centric Education, Health, etc. This needs to be broad-based, including sectors such as small cap projects, one-time projects, projects undertaken by individuals / groups, etc. by capping the funds for the sectors say, 10% or 15% of Annual Allocable Funds at the disposal of the corporate entity.

Last but not the least, CSR funds should be uniformly disbursed to the Projects, be it of capital-intensive funding or a revenue expenditure nature. Meaning thereby, Funds such as Capital-Intensive Projects, should be given from the Government's Escrow Account, to be utilized basis approval. Suitable mechanism can be devised, such as filing forms therefor & seeking approval thereon.

The main idea is to prevent frauds, diversion of funds, etc. by unscrupulous Corporates, who have vested, ulterior motives, rather than CSR.

Let's take larger picture in frame. If we were to see mushroom growth in Schools, Colleges, Universities, etc. in recent past, as compared to 50-60 years of India's independence, it will throw light on the CSR funding, by what-so-ever nomenclature, source of funding these institutions, in the name of donations, charity, etc. Under the garb of CSR, Donations, major funding is going into development of Real Estate structures, for private benefit in the hands of select few capitalist economies in the ultimate genesis, rather, the ownership should rest with the public at large. Ideally, there should be mechanism designed by the government with the support of the general public so that the benefit is not limited, rather, broad-based. This must be made for Public beneficiary, general public at large, so as to reap benefits of it in a sustainable basis.

—

CASE STUDIES → *Real Life Experienced*

Natural Disasters, Floods, etc.:

•   Dowleswaram Village, East Godavari District in Andhra Pradesh (India). Already discussed hereinabove.

https://www.indiatoday.in/magazine/indiascope/story/19860915-freak-floods-cripple-andhra-pradesh-at-least-250-people-dead-1-million-left-homeless-801215-1986-09-14

Photo: this photo is used for representation purposes only.

- My Senior, Ex-Director from Oil & Natural Gas Commission ('ONGC'), as also, the Author himself had experienced devastating Floods in the North-Eastern Region of India, mainly Assam & adjoining regions, which is quite prone to Floods, each year. Also, very recently in India's Capital - New Delhi, there was Floods, due to which some areas of the Capital were marooned.

A realistic assessment was made of the unforeseen horror unfolding, ensuing situation arisen, relief-cum-rehabilitation camps / projects set-up, food, clothing & shelter bare necessity needs met. Also, witnessed the usual course of action taken by the Local Authorities, Administration, Government Department in sync with, Co-ordination, Co-operation with the Non-Government Organizations ('NGO') & Support received from the local Public, etc.

The key point to be noted, especially from CSR perspective has been involvement of the Young generation, Voluntary Contribution made, taking Risks at the highest level, risking their lives, in relocating Old, Needy to better, safe places, negotiating through dirty

Water (where there could be dead animals, snakes, reptiles, etc.), in Night keeping vigil from predators, thief's, etc. to save the animals, people, providing them food, safety, medicines, etc. The key learning witnessing this havoc has been "**Young Generation, ideally, aged 18-25 Years**".

Serious efforts are **_inevitable_**, especially by the Governments across the Global Village, to train the Young Generation, on a war-footing pace, on purely, Voluntary basis. At the same time, they should be earmarked, identified in large number to render their services, if need arises. Now-a-days, Technology is one the best friends, tools which in a friction of seconds can do wonders. This should used, most often platform for interface with the Young Generation to get the best results.

Ever-since **2010**, **W**e _all witnessed_ **F**_ury cast by the_ **F**_loods,_ **V**_olcano,_ **H**_urricane,_ **E**_arthquakes,_ **T**_sunami,_ **F**_orest_ **F**_ires,_ **C**_ovid-19 Pandemic, etc._

Last 15 years has made us see, what our fore-fathers did not, ever, in their wildest thoughts ever dreamt of. ←—←—←—←—←—

The "Litmus Test" is coming, next 15 years (until 2040) for sure, will decide Mother Earth's survival in the next Century...unfolding before our very Eyes, each passing Day / Night →→→→→

Natural Disasters are taking a huge toll, in the most recent years. This phenomenon, uncontrolled, is rising day-by-day, with much more gravity, serious ramifications, ruining precious lives each day. This is one of the biggest areas for CSR works to address, come forward & volunteer, without any further delay, not waiting even for a single day.

No one knows the Timing, Date for the next Natural Disaster to unfold. But, will for sure ruin lives......Let's all Work in Tandem, especially, the **Next-Gen**., save "Mother Earth".

Education:
* The Author has over decades been an ardent student, mentor & a guide. The Author spent hours and hours in the field of Education.

- The most important learning has been to have real life experiences, practical exercises, etc. This not only instills, infuses learning in the right direction, at the same time, it remains for long with the learner, taught.

- In the recent past, it is experienced most often, use of Internet, Mobile phones, etc. for learning. Information Technology ('IT') applications, etc. are very useful to use for CSR Works in case the strata to be educated is in large numbers, also, those located at distant, remote location. It's not surprising that newly born children, toddlers, etc. are very fascinated, avidly use the Mobile phones, TV, etc. and *glued* for several hours.

- CSR works were experienced mostly in Children's Education, Schools, Social Skills program, etc. Teachers, mostly Females take time from their daily chores, regular teaching in the Schools, Colleges, etc. attend CSR projects, help guide, take classes there. CSR in this field not only help in preparing students face examination, etc., also, it helped in direct employment opportunity skills such as Skill Development {*Computers, Stitching Machine, Arts & Craft training programs, Food preparation, Industrial Machine training skills, etc.*} Ideally, there should be 20 to

25 number of students to be taught in any field. Also, there should be a two-way Communication (teacher-taught) to have a more effective learning.

• One classic case handled, while working in Perot Systems (now Dell). Overseas Funding was made to Indian CSR projects way back in 2008-09. The regulatory authorities, considered funding made by the Indian entity, treated on the same footing as a Foreign Fund, hence, covered under the mandatory registration under Foreign Contribution Regulation Act with the aegis of the Ministry of Home Affairs. After completing due process of law, filing compliance returns (periodical) intervals, etc., necessary CSR Project for Education in back-ward areas in Karnataka (India) were started. Due works, education, food, etc. still are done at the venue, for long. This is a sustainable CSR Project, although, with Foreign Funding (as per Indian Regulatory Authorities then). In short, the Social objective was achieved, Education, upliftment of the poor, backward areas into the mainstream, Employment opportunities were created on a large scale is really a Noble Cause. For more, visit https://www.dell.org/ideas/job-skills-training-india/

- It's been experienced teaching is much more effective by forming cluster groups in the nearby vicinity, apartments, flats, village surroundings, etc. (**a *maximum of 1 Km***) reach for the school students.

- An important learning in this direction has been element of 'Money'. Money is most important part of this CSR Project. Gone are the days when Children use to learn on bare rough pages, pencil, chalk-board, etc. Now-a-days, Computers, Audio-Video presentations, etc. are more frequently used by the student's community. Hence, for example, if a CSR Project was taken up 20 years it would have costed paltry, INR 100 / a day for 20 odd students learning. This amount will be now 1,000 / a day, or even more at constant prices, leave aside Inflation, Indexation cost, etc., nearly 10 times the cost now. The Company proposing to take-up such Projects should earmark Funds accordingly, so that the CSR works can be made sustainable, enriching, rewarding, etc. Ideally, it is most often experienced that leading Companies in the Private Sector having committed resources allocated on a regular interval / periodical, High Net-worth Individuals ('HNI') make a start, had undertaken such Projects. Most of the Companies Annual Reports, Balance Sheets,

Websites, etc. will see ***Education*** as the Thrust area, which is any Government's focus area too.

Animals Care, Feed:

- We all must have seen, witnessed in around us, on the road-sides, river-side, ponds, etc., people offering fruits, food, etc. to the animals {be it Monkeys, Cows, Dogs, Cats, Fish, Parrots, Birds, Rabbits, Dolphins, etc.}. There are often many videos circulating in the Social media, TV, Reels on YouTube, etc.

- An important learning from all these works has been, caring for Animals, who in return do not harm, are a major stress reliever, often are much passive, loving, special bonding, often adorable to feed them.

- One of the important yet, very small work often people do is to put water, milk in small bowls in around households, parks, etc. especially during, hot, summer season. Water scarcity is one of the reasons for death. Animals often source Food, but, Water is very difficult for them. In this direction, especially, in desert, remote areas where there is shortage of water, CSR Projects should be to run pooling of water, storage, etc. where potable can be placed for drinking.

• At the same time, we also must have seen people attending animals who often met with Accidents while crossing roads, forest area, nearby etc. Again, in this direction, Animal Ambulances can be of much use, beneficial, life-saving. Also, now-a-days dog bite, monkey bite, etc. menace is increasing at an alarming scale. This menace should be addressed by educating public, giving sterilization to animals, using face masks for them, etc. All these measures will certainly see a healthy growth in Animal life span & their Health.

• To make Animal care a success, Vantara project in Jamnagar, Gujarat region in India is doing a wonderful job. Similarly, several other projects are running across the Global Village to save precious life of Animals. It not helps maintain ecological balance, at the same time, saves animals, birds from extinction.

• Again, CSR projects should ideally spread awareness, set up camps, etc. in areas such as First-Aid Kits for Animals, Healthy Habits, Safety guidelines while treating Animals, feeding them, Nearby Animal Hospital details, etc. All these Works require concerted efforts of local people, as also, support from the Government (both financially, otherwise, in kind in terms of granting approval, issue of Identity Cards, co-ordination with the other NGO's, etc.).

Environmental protection:

- Very recently, on 25th March, 2025 the global giant, Casio had launched in New Delhi (India) & its adjoining areas a collection drive for recycling the Electronic Waste ('**E-waste**') generated from Home – appliances, Computers, TV, Fridge, Air-conditioners, Battery's, Chargers, etc. The CSR Project essentially has got 3 main pillars namely., the Funding (obviously, from Casio internal resources). Then, the Channel Partner associated (the CSR agency, Saint Hardyal Educational and Orphans' Welfare Society ('SHEOWS'), then comes into picture the actual spade-word, the recycling Agency → Allied Waste Solutions Pvt. Ltd. ('AWS'), whose collection Vans will take care of Waste collection from House-holds, Offices, etc., then, undertake, complete the wastage recycling. Casio has targeted collection of 3,000 Kgs of

E-waste. These efforts will in long way to reduce the harmful effects from the misuse of these wastage, at the same time, reduces pollution, aids in Environment's protection from any further degradation, etc.

•	Yet another, classic example in New Delhi region, where the Author most often spent his journey, life. There are huge heaps of garbage, landfill, etc. in earmarked locations in & around Delhi region. Over the past several decades, most of these areas kept on rising, despite recycling, etc. One of them is so huge, spread over 70-acre land, as often told as India's top most mountain of garbage {'Ghazipur'}.

Photo: this photo is used for representation purposes only.

- If we were to go some years ago, another such landfill, was converted into a beautiful park in nearby area, named Indraprastha Park (also Millennium Park), which was essentially a landfill area, totaling 84 acres land. Also, it has a World Peace Stupa, by Dalai Lama. This is another *classic* example for converting wastage into a place to enjoy evenings with family, friends, etc.

Photo: this photo is used for representation purposes only.

Others:

Students Movement- During Mandal Commission agitation movement (1990), the Author, along-with several thousand Delhi University College Students Volunteered agitated for several days, tragic immolation by a student, faced police lathi-charge, tear gas, etc. for the "reservation policy", "human rights" leading to resignation of Prime Minister then, V.P. Singh. Finally, the student's community benefitted *seeing the light of the day*.

Sports – The Author was blessed to be a part of Rhiti Group journey at initial stages of "***Mahi***" career trajectory. Making of Movie- MS Dhoni The Untold Story, which was his own story, unravel before all of us, though watched, worked, so closely alongside legendary...... Wow experience had working with Fox, several leading names to reckon with in the Industry, Corporate World.

This Group, well-known across the Global Village, is uniquely positioned, class apart and above-all, to give back to the Society in the field of Sports. At the same time, the Author had participated in a number of Community Development and Sports initiative, Press Conference, Media Conclave with Australian Cricketer- Craig McDermott, helping young Athletes, Students prepare for the Sports as a career.

These CSR works has helped guide Young Generation prepare, work for the goals, above all, remain "***Focused***" with "***Fire in the Belly***".

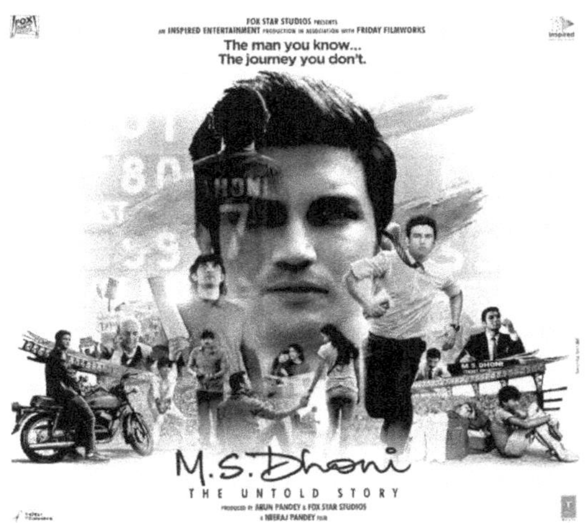

Photo: this photo is used for representation purposes only.

https://rhitigroup.com/services/

Movies- In this CSR Journey, it's been privilege, rare honour to have worked alongside leading names in the field of Movies, more particularly, Ms. Karishma Kapoor, Ms. Nimrit Kaur in their Organizations, Mentoring them.

https://en.wikipedia.org/wiki/Karisma_Kapoor

https://www.instagram.com/nimrit.kaurahluwalia/

___

CSR IN THE GLOBAL CONTEXT
{IN THE UNDERDEVELOPED / DEVELOPING / DEVELOPED ECONOMIES}

Most of the Developed Economies typically, US, Canada, UK, Australia, EU27, Brazil, Russia, Germany, etc. are saddled with typical problem of "***Carbon Footprint***". Carbon Footprint is essentially comprising of emissions from the fossil fuels, industrial production. As per reports, the wealthier a person is, the more propensity to consume, spend, etc. Again, China- a developing economy is World's top emitter of Carbon-dioxide {'Co2'}, followed by the US.

Carbon Footprint, is the direct outcome of ones spending on energy, transport, food & rest all items for his / her living in comfort. Typically, for African nations, mostly under-developed, developing stages, are having sizeable Carbon Footprint, as compared to the Developed economies. On average, in these Developed countries, the size of emission of Co2 is roughly 5,000 - 7,500 Kgs / per annum. US it's about 20,000 to 25,000 Kgs approx. / per annum.

If we were to talk about global average, it comes to roughly 4,500 to 5,000 Kgs / per annum. Its common knowledge that the level of CO2 emissions across the globe has reached alarming levels. It we were to see in India, International statistics on the subject, it not far off, since 1950 onwards there has been typically a steep, vertical elevation '***inflection***' in CO2 emission across the globe. In effect, last 70 odd years has taken a toll on each one of us life's, health, safety, environment in some form (or) other.   We all hope, candidly agree, accept this transformational shift in the world order.

Lots of international bodies are doing concerted efforts to work-out a plausible solution, find a defined road-map mitigating this menace, havoc called CO2.

Still, _as again_, we all worked in tandem fighting Covid-19 Pandemic, we need to re-energize & close this burning Co2 emissions challenge, once for all.

Now, lets devote some time on the Economies across the Global Village, how they have performed in the field of CSR. Let's understand this through some key parameters evaluated over the years, decades. This will give more clarity, sound basis to validate the figures, results, etc.

Let us now see a few stories which have made an impact in the Under- Developed / Developing / Developed Economies, as under, basis IMF statistics.
https://upload.wikimedia.org/wikipedia/commons/a/a6/Comparison_of_developed_countries.png

- **<u>Under- Developed Economies such as Sudan, Nigeria, Kenya, Gabon & host of other African Nations; Nepal, Afghanistan, Solomon Islands, etc</u>**.

Sudan- it has faced difficult times most often. CSR works aimed to reduce the involvement of the Sudanese Government, increase role by the Private Sector in the development of the Society. The Oil, Telecom & Mining Companies plays a pivot role in CSR works in Sudan. Infrastructure developments such as Schools, Water-points, Health infrastructure, etc. were taken, speeded in the efforts to develop Sudan economic health, prosperity in this region. Roads were to a large not proper, existent, hence, key thrust area for the CSR Works, especially for the Oil companies develop infrastructure. There was need felt to undertake CSR projects to help bolster local companies go global, have international presence, also benefitting in terms of profitability, marketing, repose Customer's loyalty. Also, an important aspect which remained unaddressed was legislation {focus on self-regulation, code of conduct, transparency, disseminate cultures, values amongst the masses, etc.} for the CSR framework, which the government was keen to have it in place to address. Environmental concern, betterment of social values, civil society, etc. are important, but, never been promoted in its best efforts by the Sudanese companies, whose focus predominantly remained on profits.

- **Developing Economies such as Brazil, Argentina, Botswana, South Africa, India, China, etc**.

China- the CSR initiative is restricted to the government owned companies. The focus is essentially upon protection of rights of the employees, protection of the environment, focus on quality rather than on quantity of services, goods produced.

Malaysia- Similar to China, Malaysia too follows a restricted approach. The government owned companies are legally duty bound to make CSR contribution, incur expenditure on projects such as employee's welfare (occupational health, safety, etc.). The Malaysian companies so undertaking CSR works are duty bound to report to the Stock Exchanges, whatsoever, contribution made, projects undertaken, etc. it is experienced, over the years CSR works undertaken have increased at a phenomenal pace, speed. At the Government has given it a major thrust area, in the development of the Economy. The focus remains on disclosure, transparency, accountability, ethical principles, good values, responsible business practices, sound corporate governance principles to strictly adhere & comply. Also, the thrust has been in areas of employee's welfare (gender issues, human capital development, labour legislation & welfare, health, safety); Community development (to take school, adopt it, education & such other programs); Environment (bio-fuel, waste management, endangered wildlife protection, etc.); finally, markets, to have open, yet transparent policy for supplier's engagement, social branding, adherence to sound corporate governance values, etc.

- **<u>Developed Economies such as United States of America (USA), Canada, Australia, Poland, Germany, Sweden, France, Spain, United Kingdom (UK), Italy, etc</u>**.

<u>**Australia**</u> – There has been conscious move in the direction. Also, it has added other areas for CSR, such as Human Values, Rights (laws prohibiting discrimination at work-place, conditions of work such as health, safety, etc.). There-apart, Australian companies over-reach into areas, do it on a voluntary basis, which hitherto were not mandatory. One key areas Australia stands apart from the rest is in the area of Information Technology (IT) use. It helped Old, Needy, Disabled, etc. to use, access IT services, electronic filing, financial services (banking, etc.) on more user-friendly, efficient, effective manner. Another notable feature of their CSR works has been in maintaining a healthy balance between the work- home / family life. This is very interesting, especially these days, across the global village there is serious issues, flagged often that the office times should be pruned, restricted, etc.

Australia is one of the select few countries which boasts CSR in the right ernest followed in thought-word & deed. The Companies have made policies, which strictly adhere, aimed to promote development of the community, society & protection of the environment. The underlying focus remains to build solutions for a better future for all.

One of the reports suggested, over past decade, CSR efforts have slowed. Also, an important observation to make, most companies reporting, and consistently, are the Banks, Energy sector companies. While, at the bottom were the companies loaded towards consumers services, etc. The reporting has been dismally poor, or even nil statistics on CSR.

FUTURE PERSPECTIVE

In order to develop CSR - a system driven, more inclusive & benefitting a wider spectrum of Society, Environment, the following initiatives are imperative. It will not only give impetus, scale-up CSR work in the right direction, earnest, at the same time help save the Mother 'Earth'…. Alas, already, Western Countries are _working overnight_ to find life & settle-down on Moon, Mars in times to come.

ACCOUNTABILITY:

To bring CSR benefits reaches the right person, at the right time, at the right place, the essence should be focus on accountability.

Key for any work, be it philanthropic, charity or for business, profit motivated or the like is on making any person associated in the work is held accountable, responsible, even, liable, for acts of wrong-doings, deviation, etc.

Accountability will not only help proper utilization of the funds, resources, etc., at the same time, it will also help instill confidence of the Society, Community, etc. in and around CSR Projects. Also, it helps to enhance image of the Organization in the eyes of the general public at large.

TRANSPARENCY:

It helps to repose faith of the people in the Company doing business. At the same time, it helps the Society make right choice, selection about their habits, activities, etc. whether they are correct (or) not. They are adequately informed, with adequate verifiable certification in this direction made by the Company doing CSR works. Again, there is scope for improvement basis feedback, suggestions, etc. In effect, it instills learning both for the CSR Project, as also, the Society, Community at large.... Creating, ushering win-win for both.

A leading, classic example for each one us to understand. '**Colgate-Palmolive**'. Colgate does a lot of advertising educating, promoting healthy habits amongst the general public across the globe. Its recent campaign in Hindi language "***Smile Karo Aur Shuru Ho Jaao***" has garnered lots of attention amongst public….it translates into English *__Wear your Healthy and Confident 'Smile' and Face the World with optimism, and be assured that your Smile is (PROTECTED) and cared for by Colgate, always__*". Colgate has educated the general public, at the same time been transparent in its efforts by caring for the "hygiene", thereby protecting & caring one's teeth.

LEADERSHIP:

Leadership is the '**Key**' for the success of **a**ny work → be it big (or) small.

Leader helps steer the **S**hip, in troubled times, take undue risks, focus on results, etc. to reach the destination. In effect, any CSR work success is largely dependent upon the Leadership at the helm of the affairs managing the show. The Leader should be having qualities, such as being compassionate, empathy, understanding, supporting, open-minded, creative, courageous, etc.

ETHICAL PRACTICE:

The very foundation of any CSR work is being ethical in each and every aspect, task undertaken in this work. CSR is largely a work of '*Social Activism*'. Ethical practices make things look easy, plausible. To support this point lets understand from a leading Corporate's ethical practices in this field. ITC Group, a leading name, "*treating all employees, stakeholders, and customers ethically with fairness and respect*". Again, it has advertised "*50% of total Energy would come from Renewable Sources*".

FUNDING:

The very chain for any business, non-business, not-for-profit activity (or) the like revolves around "Money". Money is the central, driving force for any activity, be it big or small. It's true, Money is scarce, which obviously creates a Demand. Money should be utilized most sparingly, in case of utmost need basis only.

All efforts go in vain, (dust bin), had there been no fully assured, verifiable sources for funding available with the Company undertaking CSR work. At the same time, it is essential that the Projects undertaken are completed with minimum possible budget, not going **over-board**.

EXPANSION OF CSR FRAMEWORK:

It's all the more important that the CSR framework MUST be expanded. Lets first identify the CSR framework. In the words of noted Carroll, CSR framework for any business rests on 4 fundamental responsibilities, duties. He has captured these pillars in the form of a Pyramid structure. Economic responsibilities are at rock bottom. Then follows, Legal responsibilities, then, Ethical responsibility. At the top most, _skewed_ portion of the ladder lies, Philanthropic responsibilities {being a Good Corporate Citizen}.

There-apart, to have a meaningful, workable, plausible approach towards making our "Mother Earth" _Live another 100 Years_ → with grace, the CSR legal framework, horizon, sphere needs to be expanded without any second thought.

CSR framework must cover, include in its ambit works such as (_those people, individuals, groups, etc. who are_ *imparting Education, providing training courses for Employment in support functions such as Computers training, Culinary works such as food preparation, Decoration, using Stitching Machine, Musical instruments, Singing, etc.) (helping the people, Animals, save Environment, both by giving money, non-monetary benefits (or) otherwise in kind, etc.) (acting as Channel Partners, supporting the Corporates in CSR, but, not on-board with them)* as a Social Service, Charitable work and a ***host of works in our day-to-day lives already discussed hereinabove, rendered by the Non-corporate Entities such as by the Individuals, association of persons, House-holds, House-wife's {working in times of recess, leisure at home, etc.}***. to be treated as a part-and-parcel of the CSR activity by the regulatory authorities (or) the like across the globe instead limiting the benefits, responsibility to only Corporates.

It's important that a suitable framework is prepared, making different attributes, yardstick, etc. to qualify a particular work, activity undertaken under CSR.

In short, why should all Corporates only have the benefits earmarked for them by the regulatory authorities, as also, exposure to public platforms garnering huge fan following, raising of funds, promoting their own brands, image, etc.

Rather, everyone, undertaking, doing the same work, should also so benefit and be a part & parcel of the CSR Journey across the Globe. On an equal footing, equal opportunity, equal treatment, equal recognition, etc. under their respective country's territories, or the like. To quote, for example, anyone, individual, etc. who is making a voluntary Contribution to identified Charitable Projects are given tax-break, tax-benefit across the global village. In India, this benefit can be availed under section 80-G of the Income Tax Act, 1961. On similar footing, equal treatment should be given in CSR.

———

SUMMARY

My aim, ultimate goal through this Book is to tap vast segment of the Society, NGO's, NextGen Professionals, Corporates, Students, Government, Investors' community or the like. To armour, equip, prepare them for umpteen challenges, especially, in area of NBR TODAY's CSR JOURNEY GLOBALLY, hitherto unheard, unexplored in the new age, rapidly changing corporate scenario, culture, most-difficult age for corporate world, yet, for betterment of Society, truly reflective of Social Order- a stable state of the society, peace, tranquility, etc.

In India, erstwhile Companies Act, 1956 did not mandate any specific instances, conditions, circumstances requiring any compliance, contribution by the Corporate entities.

Only in a select few instances, when occasioned at the behest of Companies, CSR was made primarily to ensure better image, garner support, avail benefits from the government in some form or other, etc.

However, there were handful, meagre, selective instances of NBR TODAY's CSR JOURNEY GLOBALLY, most often at the instance of the Leading Corporate Houses across the global village such as Gates Foundation, Tata Trusts, etc. Also, there was paltry contribution of other Corporates (not sizeable proportion to that of the Leading Corporate Houses, etc.) They often used the CSR contribution either for religious purposes, leadership family legacy aspirations, etc.

With changing times, adopting more pragmatic approach, ushered new era under the Companies Act, 2013 regime. Under new Act, provisions identified especially projects which necessarily are forming a part and parcel of the CSR Project framework which is compliance of law, not otherwise.

Across the global village, in Canada, UK, Australia, Singapore, etc. too had seen the CSR framework working for over decades, a few stock exchanges (social) were started, but, did not survive, live to the aspirations of the market, hence, were closed. This framework of Social Stock Exchanges, has started showing good results, atleast in Indian context. There are few numbers of

Companies registered therein, availing funding from the public for social cause, works, etc. The amount is not sizeable, still, there is need for marketing, more involvement of the public to really understand the true benefit of "**Listed**" company in a Social Stock Exchange, Government Subsidy Schemes, etc. to make this platform a real success story, for the world the emulate across the Global Village.

In India, new Section 135 placed under statute has now taken care of all these situations under "compulsory" & "voluntary" route for NBR TODAY's CSR JOURNEY GLOBALLY. There are a number of rules, regulations, circulars, notifications, clarifications, etc. issued in the subject by the MCA.

https://www.mca.gov.in/content/mca/global/en/acts-rules/ebooks/acts.html?act=NTk2MQ==#Corporate_Social_Responsibility

Now, under the new regime, we are going to see a larger number of companies making compliance, which didn't exist earlier. This process will not only help present a realistic position of the state of affairs of the social fabric, social values, social culture to maintaining social order within the Country & at same time, it will also help corporates in endeavor to be better Corporate Citizen by adhering Corporate Governance in right ernest, in its true spirit.

———

KEY TAKEAWAYS

In our initial discussion, we reposed confidence that we all will unravel, unearth NBR TODAY's CSR JOURNEY GLOBALLY aim to **_walk the talk_**, pin-point specific areas of concern, looking for plausible answers, finding a defined, yet, definite solution that too in a few minutes, hours, days.

Let us now work-out, address these "Key" task of our Journey across the Global Village to **_Make it a better place for YOU and for ME and for the entire HUMAN RACE_** →→→→→→→→ Quoted from MJ song, Heal the World, my Childhood Love, Hero.

- ACCOUNTABIITY:

Accountability is one of the several aspects important for any CSR Project to unfold into a CSR Journey.

- MONEY:

Money (or) Money's worth, in kind, or otherwise, has {ALWAYS BEEN} the driving force for any activity, how small (or) big, economic (or) non-economic, Social Responsibility work is no exception, to start, make it sustainable, into a CSR Journey.

- ETHICS:

Principles of Ethical behavior should be imbibed as a part of life, running through the CSR works seamlessly, without any force, external interference (or) requiring audit to validate it.

- COLLABORATION:

In case, the CSR Projects are not having adequate resources (men, money, material, etc.), but, there is urge, need to work on it, then, possible collaboration can be made with those who are working on the same, or willing to fund them or the like. This concept if developed in the right ernest with government impetus, it will create lots of opportunities still unexplored, untapped due to various reasons, corruption, no keenness to contribute for obvious self-centric, vested interest, etc. are a few deterrents to be overcome soon.

- TECHNOLOGY:

It's always good to use, benefit from Artificial Intelligence, Information technology platform, etc. This will not only save lot of invaluable time, cost, but at the same time helps to be abreast with the latest technology advancements (***Examples:* in Medical treatment of the Patients virtually by the Doctors, in Court's {virtual hearing assistance are a way of life, especially, after Covid-19 Pandemic, which will help the poor, needy, woman, etc. as a social cause benefitting the Society at large}** *in Education classes online for the Poor, under-privileged across the Global Village is accessible with laptop, mobiles, classrooms, anywhere, even in the inner-most, remote areas of Villages, etc*.)

- TRANSPARENCY:

Transparency is one of the key aspects for both the doer, as well as the outside world to vouch it, take a leaf out of the experiences had in the CSR Journey & save time in taking up the next project. It also instills confidence of the regulatory authorities, public at large, etc. especially where the is need for funding from external sources, most often, as also enhances the reputation, image of the Business per-se.

- COMMUNITY:

The focus should ideally be "Community centric", such as local village, township, city limits in around the businesses. Also, in these areas, cluster groups, more predominantly, Education Institutions such as the Schools, Colleges, or Industrial training institutions, Skills Development initiatives, Computer training institutions, etc. are a key.

- ABUSES, TRIVIAL QUARREL, etc.:

There-apart, focus can be made on the Elderly, Homeless, drugs, Alcohol, cigarettes, tobacco, etc. rampant abuses amongst Young generation, poor, etc. in the recent 5 odd years, as per verifiable sources. **Example**: one thought running across my mind has been reels, video's going viral on WhatsApp, YouTube, Social media platforms, etc. showing road rage, accidents, brawl (*religious reasons, encroachment over land*), house-hold fight, quarrel, Mall areas, across crowded Railway Stations, Bus depots, Metro Stations, etc. Ideally suggested to have non-police teams, in uniform, such as in India, we see National Cadet Corps (NCC), Marshals (both Male & Female), etc. rendering invaluable services, with the aid, assistance of the local police, local authorities, etc.

- **PARA-MEDICAL HELP:**

Another class could be attending those in medical need, attention, etc. such as Road-side, Accident victims, those requiring medical attention such as at the Airports, Railway Stations, Bus Stations, etc. Apart from Humans, similarly, focus on Animals too can be useful. Last but not the least, groups can be formed to work on projects to protect the Environment, clean water, planting trees, removing trash, wastage in public areas, creating awareness program to educate public about them, etc.

- **TRIVIAL SOCIAL WORKS:**

There are many projects still unexplored for CSR such as removal of unnecessary posters, political advertisement for election, religious purposes, etc. damaging the environment, surroundings, walls, road-side, beautification of the city, towns & its adjoining areas, etc. The help of local authorities, municipal department, etc. can be of much use in this effort to remove the posters, also, another team can work to canvass, educate the public & others about the harmful effects.

- **RESTORE MISPLACED, LOST TO THEIR FAMILY:**

There-apart, there are other projects such as kidnapping / abduction / trafficking, misguided youth, girls, old people leaving their homes in search of jobs, home unrest, quarrel, etc. with assistance of the local police, local authorities, education institutions, etc. In India, the statistics are alarming, fearful. Every 30 seconds, there is a person (child, girl, old, etc.) is not at his home, runs-away, quarrel, education, employment need, drugs abuse, trafficking, etc. Global Village,

- **LEADERSHIP:**

Last but not the least, it goes without saying, CSR Works, most often, demands that the Leadership should rest with person of "Humane Values", "Eminence" with qualities of Respect for others, Demeanor, Love, Compassion, Modesty, Self-respect, Ethical behavior, Equality, Open-minded, Integrity, Creativity, Morality, Honesty, Being Responsible & being Tolerant. In this direction, as per verifiable sources, to our public knowledge, a few names that cross our minds are **_Mother Teresa, Mahatma Gandhi, Nelson Mandela, Winston Churchill, Dalai Lama, Narendra Modi, Martin Luther King Jr., Oprah Winfrey, Harib Al Kitani, Swami Vivekanand, Julius Nyerere, Bill Gates, Yasir Al-Rumayyan, Eleanor Roosevelt, etc._**, this list is going on expanding, each day………………………… these all individuals {institutions in themselves}, each of them had service to mankind, social upliftment, save Mother Earth, as their foremost Love to do, perform in each breath they took.

In brief, of all the points majorly taking forward CSR Journey in the right ernest, the Leadership stands apart which is the only, only driving force behind success of CSR works, to make it a sustainable….CSR Journey in India, globally.

———

CONCLUDING REMARKS

The Author is blessed to be constantly under careful hands.

Indeed, it's an *h*onour to be in company, associated with accomplished individuals, most often-luminaries {political dispensation, top-notch government officials, Senior Advocates, Leading Corporate Leaders, Founders of IIM-Ahmedabad, etc.} & able to present theirs, his own perspective before you all.

A *BIG WARM THANK YOU ALL!*

My idea is to study & present NBR TODAY's CSR JOURNEY GLOBALLY, its evolution, most recent developments in the future all these works culminated in a simple, easy to read & understandable formatted language.

Focus was to address especially to NGO's, Corporate citizens, Professionals, Educators, Students, Government, importantly the general public need at large in the present age which is myriad in sufferings, agony, etc. having important ramifications. It will generate their enthusiasm, interest, reading skills, equip themselves to face umpteen challenges in this complex, ever-changing corporate working in a dynamic environment, evolving global scenario.

Dear students, professionals, general public, NGO's, Corporates, etc. you all are welcome to contribute in whatsoever manner your goodself wishes can make as a part & parcel of this enviable Journey. Also, can reach me on naveenbhatnagar27@gmail.com +91 9810224073 (WhatsApp); 8130839020 https://nbrtodays.webnode.com

The main idea & focus of this book has been to generate interest, enthuse creativity, passion amongst the researchers, students, academicians, NGO's, leading Corporate Houses, CSR Foundations such as Reliance Foundation, Michael & Susan Foundation, etc. more importantly, the Corporate World with the nuances of NBR TODAY's CSR JOURNEY GLOBALLY.

It helps gain valuable insights about its purpose, intent, usefulness amongst the Corporates, NGO's, spread across the length & breath of India, with their over-reach globally.

My goal is to make NBR TODAY's CSR JOURNEY GLOBALLY a way of life, a more useful tool equipped in the Corporate's armour, hitherto, not provided.

This tool here are a catalyst for change, should be used, more sparingly, effectively, efficiently to be a better Corporate Citizen, thereby providing, attaining highest values enshrined for creation & maximization of shareholders value, wealth & in end legacy to cherish.

I have tried to explain the nuances of NBR TODAY's CSR JOURNEY GLOBALLY much more on Voluntary CSR Funding the Projects (which is the norm across the global village, most often) for social cause {but, not Economic Value addition} from a holistic perspective.

With the changing times, it is the need of the hour that Corporates, re-invent using 'KEY TAKEAWAYS' given elsewhere in this text-book by being an altruist, making pragmatic approach, instead of adopting a lop-sided, myopic, cynical approach funding their own cause, benefit.

Obviously, NBR TODAY's CSR JOURNEY GLOBALLY is going to unleash growth in the jobs for specialized professionals {MBA, Advanced Diploma Courses, specialized courses in social work, etc.} in times to come, rather than staff handling clerical mundane jobs, work such as typing, editing, generating reports, etc. With this and many such newer frontiers forging, making in-roads for professionals, students, academicians. Think _out of_

<u>box</u> spreading wings across domestic domain, to other regions, frontiers, etc. un-explored, untapped, rather limiting such works to government to handle, especially in Metropolitan, Cities, etc.

There is one gray area which is needed to be addressed at the right earnest, which is the need of the hour. Corporates, most often, give CSR a second consideration vis-à-vis its compliances or the like. This needs to be addressed, corrected, as Voluntary CSR projects undertaking, funding NGO those earmarked social cause projects is a matter of concern.

Hitherto, correction was felt appropriate necessarily due to non-compliance, defaults emanated at behest of NGO team's collusion and / or Corporate itself. For sure, this mistake will be addressed with strict enforcement of law, in India, globally, compliance at the highest pedestial (Parliament in case of India), etc. Hope, we all are on same page on this aspect.

In era of globalization, paradigm shifts, socio-political considerations, etc. the pace at which CSR is evolving, emerging, changing is really faster than expected, perceived by the law makers, NGO's, Corporates, its practitioners.

Sadly, especially for ones studying CSR, then, if he / she chooses to practice it in its true letter & spirit, it becomes challenging to understand what-is, what-was, what-will be perceived {'how fast', holds the 'key'} with plethora of compliance to address, government notifications, circulars, on top of its seminars, articles & articles or the like!

Sounds Great isn't, but, at what Cost?

It is really not far off when we will see a time, transitional shift, people's movement see the light of the day, reporting, funding at door-steps, more confidence reposed, etc. will see the light of the day.

If all things go on smoothly, the enabling e-forms reporting for CSR in India would be processed and taken on record then, rather than, through the extant lengthy, taxing, cumbersome legal process under NBR TODAY's CSR JOURNEY GLOBALLY, albeit, non-existent, non-prevalent a few years ago altogether. Similarly, the Global

Village jurisdiction regulator suggest processes that are easy, system friendly, etc. so that reporting is done seamlessly, without any deterrent, bureaucratic hassles.

Really!! Sounds crazy isn't!! But we all are positive!!

By now, you should have fair estimate of your skill level in comparison to the others. This work culminated, oriented as a Ready Reckoner / Digest / Guide, should definitely push your understanding from an intermediate level to becoming an expert on emerging area of legal jargon more particularly on Voluntary, Mandatory CSR reporting, especially, in the Annual Reports, presentations made to the potential investors such Private Equity (PR) Funding, in the Directors Report or the like. Those Companies / groups show-casing good work, for a social cause brings benefit to the Society, Environment at large.

Consistent effort, persistence, utmost faith, belief in self & service to the mankind, human race, flora-fauna are the key to success for any CSR Project's *enviable journey*. If you feel that understanding newly introduced concept NBR TODAY's CSR JOURNEY GLOBALLY its enabling thought perceived by the law makers (in India, especially), concepts, techniques, has advanced your skills, would really appreciate & earnestly, humbly request your good selves to make it a ***daily habit*** to understand different facets of emerging challenges faced by Corporates in the emerging global order, which the Author has bitter experienced (CSR) for over 3 decades, *on Board*, working with them as a Company Secretary, Head-Legal, etc.

Do learn newer insights, techniques, articulate ideas with your peer group which will certainly help enhance your skills, understanding on this emerging topic of debate.

Finally, I would like to express my deep gratitude that you spent your time reading, learning NBR TODAY's CSR JOURNEY GLOBALLY skills in this book. Above everything else, I value your precious time. The ultimate goal of any good work should be to save, not take, your time.

By working through this work, Naveen firmly believes your esteem must have gained sharp insights about NBR TODAY's CSR JOURNEY GLOBALLY its enabling benefits especially to the Corporate World, techniques, etc. in a positive approach, obviously, as a law-abiding corporate citizen.

Also, you should have experienced a definite positive return on invaluable time invested & your hard-earned money.

<u>Naveen Heartily Thanks You All for your Understanding</u>!

Now, please keep investing in yourself & stay active with my number of NBR Today® authored works.

Om Sai Ram